MINSTERWORT

IN

OLD PHOTOGRAPHS

Compiled by

John Jenner
Ronnie Knight
Anthony Lynch
Terry Moore-Scott

Published by
The Minsterworth Community History Project
in conjunction with the Minsterworth Village Hall
Tel: 01452 750160 or 01452 750136

Compiled by
John Jenner
Ronnie Knight
Anthony Lynch
Terry Moore-Scott

ISBN 13 978-0-9554410-0-4

ISBN 10 0-9554410-0-5

Front cover:
Detail from a picture of the Minsterworth 'bobby' riding his beat on the frozen
River Severn during the big freeze of 1940.
(By kind permission of the Gloucester Citizen)

Back cover
Flooded river bank with daffodils.The Naight, Minsterworth.
(By kind permission of Dr Anthony Lynch)

This publication was supported by a grant from
the National Lottery 'Awards for All' scheme.

Net proceeds from the sale of this book will go towards
improvements at the Minsterworth Village Hall.

Printed by
Stoate & Bishop (Printers) Ltd Cheltenham

Contents

Introduction

Over half a century of Minsterworth's past and present and changing history comes to life in this first small book of your photographs. Taken mostly between the 1890's and 1950's, villagers have searched and dusted off old albums and rooted amongst forgotten boxes in their lofts to find them.

The pictures show the timeless realities - the constant cycles of the seasons and the weather, the River Severn and its tides. Meanwhile successive generations of Minsterworth people have almost unconsciously adapted to changes in their domestic and working lives as the old order of the world has more rapidly changed around them.

There are other glimpses of the past: of F W Harvey, whose poems so often captured in a line the atmosphere of old Minsterworth and the views around it:

> *"The river flows, the blossom blows in orchards by the river. "*

Farmers and their machinery, the roads and transport along them, houses and their occupants, the school and its scholars - these and village events and much more are caught by camera. Bold faces in war time, and smiling faces in peace time shine out from the pages.

We believe that these photographs do more than provide a mere record of this unique English village. They bring its history alive again and evoke the very spirit of the villagers themselves.

We hope that you enjoy the book as much as we did compiling it.

John Jenner
Ronnie Knight
Anthony Lynch
Terry Moore-Scott

I

The Seasons

Winter

Minsterworth Village Hall under a carpet of winter snow

Kale for winter feed being taken across the main road to Elm Farm in the 1950s. Brian Browning is thought to be driving the old tractor and Graham Watkins is standing on the trailer.

With winter-time comes Christmas and all its festivities. This charming scene is of the full cast of Minsterworth School's nativity play which took place in the village hall back in 1954.

Winter 1940 brought dramatic scenes to the River Severn at Minsterworth when thick ice was broken up by a high tidal bore. (Photograph by courtesy of the Gloucester Citizen)

And then the floods. This photograph, taken in January 1960 near Oakle Street, looks up the A48 towards Gloucester after the river had overflowed its bank at Plackett Pool. The house on the right was the home of Bert Prosser, the village's blacksmith, builder and undertaker for many years. That on the left, called Bodnum's Cottage, was demolished shortly after this picture was taken to allow for road widening.

Spring

High spring tide at The Naight

Pear blossom at Elmore.

Spring at last. Daffodils in profusion at Minsterworth Court where Mrs Margaret Vyner Ellis lived until her death in 1958. She won many awards for her daffodils and reportedly grew one which carries her name.

The late-Spring church festival of Rogation-tide is traditionally when church-goers look forward to having good crops in the season ahead. At St Peter's Minsterworth, as on this occasion in May 1949, Rogation services were often held out of doors on the near-by river bank. The gentleman on the far left of the picture facing away from the camera is Mr David East, a churchwarden at the time.

Every year in early Spring, great shoals of elvers came up the river on the tide and were caught by their thousands in home-made nets. In this tranquil scene, photographed in 1940, Minsterworth church tower can just be seen on the left.

Summer

Doreen Clifton and Mrs Dyer manning a stall at the village hall fete in 1967

The Minsterworth Horticultural Show and Fete used to be a regular summer-time event with its displays of flowers, fruit and vegetables, ever-popular stalls, fancy dress competitions and games for the children. Here from the 1920s are the Rev Charles Oldfield Bartlett, vicar of St Peter's, and his niece, beside the heavily-laden sweet stall.

One summer around 1930 a village Bathing Beauty Competition was held to raise funds for the Village Hall and, as this picture shows, it attracted a considerable number of entries all attired in the latest bathing styles of the day. The group on the right, presumably the panel of judges, includes the Rev. Bartlett and Mrs Margaret Vyner Ellis. (Photograph courtesy of the Gloucester Citizen)

Dating from around 1900 is this carefully posed photograph of a group of haymakers taken during a break in their labours (the man in the centre is obviously pouring himself a drink of cider or ale from a flagon under his arm). The lettering on the front of the wagon reads "Henry Barrett, Minsterworth, Gloucestershire"; a farmer of this name is listed in the 1901 census for Minsterworth.

The Dog at Over Inn used to arrange summer charabanc trips for their patrons, many of whom came from Minsterworth. Here we see an impressive all-male group of trippers with their chauffer-driven charabanc while on a visit to Gough's Caves at Cheddar in the early 1920s.

Autumn

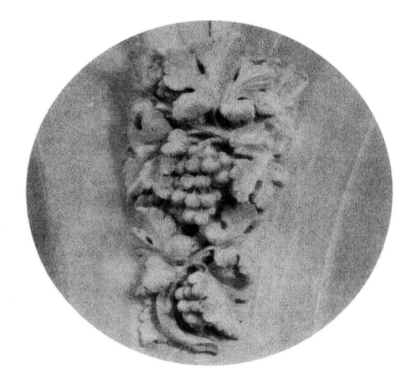

Stone carving of vine and grapes in St Peter's church Minsterworth

In Minsterworth, autumn harvesting of apples (in this case destined for cider making) was often a family affair, as this highly picturesque scene from the early 1900s shows. Note in particular the man on the right using the traditional long "lug" pole to shake down the fruit and, in the background, the unhitched pony trap that transported the family to and from the orchard.

For centuries, the growing of apples and pears for cider and perry making was a major industry locally with virtually every farm and small holding having its own cider press. This old photograph, the original of which carries the caption "Ready For Fruit", shows three Minsterworth cider men, all members of the Greening family (Tom, Bert and Bill), preparing to deal with the newly harvested fruit.

Another apple havest scene, this time showing dessert apples being taken from the tree.

This celebration of the harvest by a group of infants from Minsterworth School is believed to date from around 1954.

2

The River

The Severn Bore just upstream of Minsterworth

Judging by the length of this line of cars parked on the main road in the 1920s, The Dinney must have been a popular place with visitors coming to watch the bore.

A more tranquil view of the river and the main road at The Dinney around 1930 with a 'stop-me-and-buy-one' ice-cream seller on his tricycle.

During the big freeze of 1940, thick ice on the River Severn made it possible for Minsterworth's "bobby" P.C. Hector Evans to cycle to the very limit of his territory which ran down the middle of the river. Mrs Beatrice Webb, of Snowdrop Cottage, and Mrs Clarice Mayo and her husband Stan (in the trilby) look on with amusement. (Reproduced courtesy of the Gloucester Citizen).

Another scene of the river iced over, this time at the old Salmon Inn ferry. Landlord of the Salmon, Walter Wellington, pulls his grandson Keith Smith on a sled towards the Minsterworth bank. Also trying out the ice are George 'Joker' Bennett and his brother from Elmore and Colin Price of Pershbrook in Minsterworth. (Reproduced courtesy of the Gloucester Citizen)

In 1948, following earlier flooding at Plackett Pool, a concrete flood barrier was installed on the river bank just down from Pershbrook Cottage (seen in the far left of the picture) and the hope was that it would be an adequate defence ....

.... and at first the barrier held out but it was no match for the bad floods of 1960. The building on the left is the old fish house at Plackett Pool and across the river is Elmore Back Farm.

...... but the flood of 1960 eventually receded and traffic could pass on the A48 again - but not without difficulty, as the motorist in the foreground found. In this picture, looking towards Gloucester, the former Grange Hotel is seen on the left. (Reproduced courtesy of the Gloucester Citizen)

3

People and Events

Mrs Margaret Vyner Ellis photographed at a Minsterworth Horticultural Show
sometime during the 1920s

A portrait believed to be of Wintour Stephens, Minsterworth church's last parish clerk, who resided at The Naight. His service as parish clerk, a post he still held in 1908, lasted for over 25 years.

Godfrey William Viner Ellis, the first elected chairman of Minsterworth Parish Council after it was formed in 1894. He died in 1911 aged 47, leaving his wife Margaret and two children. (Reproduced by kind permission of the Glos. Rec. Office)

In 1890, Howard Harvey (shown here c.1900) moved to Minsterworth from Hart-pury with his wife Matilda to set up home at Parlours Farm, later known as The Redlands. There, and until his death in 1909, he farmed and bred great shire horses; he also served as school governor and parish councillor. His eldest son Will was the poet F W Harvey.

The Harvey family at The Redlands in 1910. Will is sitting front right and his mother Matilda (or 'Tillie' as she was known in the family) is seated at the centre of the group.

Mrs Margaret Vyner Ellis in 1914 showing off her sporty up-to-the-minute auto-
mobile which, in the absence of her husband who had died three years earlier, she
probably drove herself.

Some of the fashionable guests (including probably the Dean of Gloucester) enjoying a reception in the garden of Minsterworth Court in 1926 following the wed-
ding of Margery Viner and the Rev. Wilfred Armstrong. Afterwards the couple set
up home at nearby Cray Croft cottage.

Charlie Trigg - the jockey. Charlie was born at Minsterworth in 1881 and for a time lived at the White House. His subsequent riding career won him fame and international success, his fearless riding style earning him the nickname "Hell for Leather Charlie". His best-known feat was in 1902 at Edinburgh when he rode five winners in a single day.

From a different Trigg family was Mrs Catherine Trigg who lived with her three children at Bodnum's Cottage. Throughout the 1920s and 1930s, she took in washing from the 'big houses' around Minsterworth. In this photograph (taken around 1950) Mrs Trigg is with her little grand-daughter Peggy.

On 29 November 1928 the Minsterworth Village Hall (or Memorial Hall as it was first known) was formally opened by the Duchess of Beaufort. She is shown here approaching the hall accompanied by Mrs Vyner Ellis and the Rev. C. O. Bartlett, vicar of Minsterworth, and Mrs Bartlett. The Guard of Honour was mounted by the 1st Minsterworth Company of Girl Guides holding staves to form an arch.

In 1928, a new road was opened to improve access from the main road to the Wesleyan chapel at Calcotts Green. Here we see Mrs Vyner Ellis in her car inaugurating the route which is now the drive-way to Chapel House.

A man and his pony. This is Mr John Messenger, husband of the village postmistress.

For many years, Mrs Mary Maria Messenger was the village postmistress occupying Graingers cottage which served as a telephone exchange. She died in 1936 and was succeeded by Miss Isabel Messenger, her daughter.

For parishioners of St Peter's in the early 1940s, tending to the churchyard was a group activity. Making up the group in this photograph are (left to right): - ? -, Arthur Price, Johnnie Russell, Sid Pugh, Moses Roberts (with white beard), Tom Phelps, Stan Mayo, (Bob) Selwyn, - ? -, Bert Prosser, Fred Boyce, Bill Pugh, the Rev. Mr Brockwell, Donald Boyce, Charlie Butt, Harold Boyce and Fred Webb (boy with scythe).

A Minsterworth British Legion dinner probably at the Grange Hotel sometime during the 1940s. Present in this photograph are (left to right): front row - Mr East, Mr Brown, - ? -, Bert Evans, Ted Webb, Thomas Phelps; back row - Fred Ayland, Bob Selwyn, Jim Meadows, Fred Boyce, Bert Prosser, 'Joker' Bennett, - ? -, Mr Phillips.

A bevy of young mothers and their children attending the baby clinic in Minsterworth Village Hall at Christmas time 1950. The formidable-looking nurse in charge is believed to be Nurse Teague and the group includes many well-known faces, including Jane Prosser with Susan and Joan Prosser with Ann.

Inspecting the goodies for sale at a Minsterworth fete in the 1960s are (from left to right): Mrs A Phelps, - ? -, R Leach, P Meadows, T Greening and P Meadows.

4

Places

Minsterworth Village Hall shortly after completion in 1928. Note the end of the loggia, or verandah, that ran along the north wall where today the British Legion room stands

The present parish church of St. Peter's, with its familiar turreted tower, was built in 1870 to replace the ancient church which had stood on this river-side site since medieval times. The churchyard contains many old gravestones and several fine table-top tombs commemorating Minsterworth families from the 18th and early 19th centuries.

Although not in our parish, St Andrew's Church at Churcham, and the view of its distinctive continental-style tower, are very familiar to everyone in Minsterworth. The appearance of today's church however is the result of major restoration in 1878 after a disastrous fire three years before. This very early photograph shows the condition of the church after the fire.

Minsterworth's Wesleyan Methodist Chapel was erected on the bank above
Calcotts Green in 1845 and served as a place of non-conformist worship for well over
100 years. Due to dwindling congregations it closed in the 1970s and was demolished
soon after. This picture of the chapel being taken down shows the roundel set in the wall
high above the door which reads "WESLEYAN CHAPEL 1845".

Old "Chapel House" in Calcotts Green in the early 1900s, showing members of the
Hurcombe family who lived there then. For many years the Hurcombes were
caretakers of the Wesleyan Chapel, part of the back of which can be seen on the
left. Today the house, much altered, is known as Chapel Cottage.

This small Minsterworth cottage, still occupied in the 1890s, was demolished many years ago along with its great chimney. Note the men's large reaping hooks and the wide bonnet that women wore as they worked in the fields.

The Mitchell family at Pound Cottage around 1900. The cottage, now derelict, still stands on the corner at the top of Pound Lane; so too does the small road-side stall on the opposite corner where the family used to sell fruit and vegetables.

Among Minsterworth's listed old buildings is Street End Cottage, parts of which date from the 17th century. This picture postcard view, dating from around 1925, shows the cottage still with its traditional thatched roof. Just beyond is Snowdrop Cottage, another listed building from the 17th century.

Until 1964 when it was demolished for road widening, Bodnum's Cottage, seen here, stood on the north side of the main road just east of the junction with Oakle Street Lane. In common with a number of older river-side houses, large parts of Bodnum's were constructed of black slag blocks brought up-river mostly from the copper works at Bristol.

During the 19th and part of the 20th centuries, Duni House was the principal home of the Viner Ellis and later the Viner Brady families. It later became the Grange Hotel but was demolished in the 1960s. Today, all that remains of this once imposing early Victorian property is a part of the original garden wall and one or two mature trees.

This elegant wing of old Minsterworth Court, shown as it appeared in 1967, was built in Georgian times. According to the builder's accounts of the time, it cost all of 15 guineas to build. A number of Minsterworth's prominent families have been associated with it, including the Ellis, Hawkins and Viner Ellis families.

Originally, access to the village hall and nearby tennis courts was via these steps and gateway which stood beside the main road opposite Bury Lane. An indentation in the present-day retaining wall facing the road marks where the gate was.

Beyond the gateway was a sunken pathway (now filled in) which led to the village hall basement entrance and, up further steps, to the loggia at the back. This photograph, taken just after the hall was built in 1928, shows the layout of the site and members of the Greening family taking the air.

THE FARM CAFE

Minsterworth,
Glos.

Tel: Minsterworth 271

From well before the war and into the eighties, the Farm Cafe on the main road was a popular teashop for travellers and local residents alike. It was finally demolished in 1997 and the site is now occupied by Home Orchard bungalow.

The Apple Tree Inn, Minsterworth, near Gloucester.

The oldest part of the Appletree Inn is believed to date back to the 17th century when it was probably a farm building. After having a variety of uses, it appears not to have become a public house until well into the 1900s. From the model of car in the forecourt, this photograph was probably taken in the 1950s, if not earlier.

5

Minsterworth
At Work

From the 1930s is this photograph of Mr Charles Mogg and Mr Fred Vaux with Mr
Mogg's pedigree Friesian bull

Apple harvesting in Minsterworth sometime during the early 1900s. The way in which the fruit is piled up and being scooped into sacks seems to indicate that it was destined for cider making.

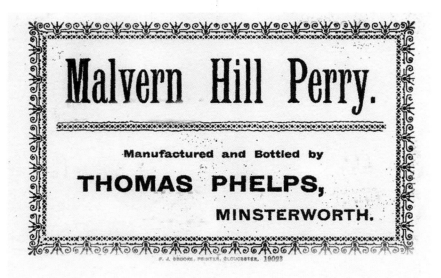

They say that Thomas Phelps of Minsterworth made excellent perry cider from locally grown 'Malvern Hill' pears. He operated from a large cider barn at Lyn Paddock and, during the 20s and 30s, he was known for being the only local cider producer possessing a motor lorry for his deliveries. This is a copy of one of his bottle labels from that time. (Reproduced by kind permission of Gloucestershire Record Office)

In addition to being a cider merchant, Thomas Phelps (with help from his family and friends) could also turn his hand to haymaking and building a haystack. His cider delivery lorry, on which he is standing (far right), came in handy as a haywain. The writing on the lorry's cab door reads: "Thomas Phelps, Cider Merchant, Minsterworth, Glos'shire".

Haymaking on a hot summer day makes this cider break especially welcome; note the man on the far right pouring cider from a barrel under his arm. The writing on the waggon reads: "William Selwyn, Minsterworth, Gloucestershire", quite probably the W. Selwyn recorded as occupying Elm Farm around 1910.

Farmer Charlie Harris of Duni Farm turning hay in the field across the road from Severn Bank in the early 1950s. The boy at the reins is Richard Fullbrook-Leggatt whose family lived at Severn Bank House at the time.

Long net fishing in the river at Minsterworth around the early 1900s. The long net consisted of a sheet of netting up to 200 yards long which was paid out across the river by punt and then pulled in with its catch. The wooden slatted staging (called a 'flake') was laid on the river-side beach to give firm footing for the fishermen.

A crew of at least four men was required for long net fishing: one (the "debut man") to hold one end of the net on shore, two on the punt letting out the net into the river and a fourth (the "muntle man") on either the same or opposite bank to secure the other end of the net. Here we see the two ends of the net being hauled in with the catch.

The same long net crew as above (minus one) taking a break on the river bank at Madams Pool. Two of the characters have been identified as Thomas Phelps and "Poof" Spiers.

6

Minsterworth
At Play

Picnic tea after a cricket match between Minsterworth ladies and gentlemen in 1938.
The match was probably played on the Churcham club's ground at Oakle Street

Minsterworth Band Of Hope temperance group setting out on a children's outing in 1920. The right-hand lady standing before the wagonette is Miss Annie Stephens who was Sunday School teacher at the local Wesleyan chapel.

One of the attractions at the Minsterworth Fruit, Flower and Vegetable Show held in the grounds of The Court in 1927 entailed fishing for ducks floating in a bath of water.

Will Harvey, the poet, was also an excellent footballer and cricketer and was captain of Minsterworth AFC in 1910 when this picture of the team was taken. The club, of which he was a founder member, celebrates its centenary in 2007. Back row: I Prosser, E Coleman, C Prosser, E Hurcombe, W Messenger, I Greening and A Artus; seated: I Russell, Will Harvey and H Russell.

Minsterworth AFC, here photographed outside its H.Q., the Appletree Inn, were the champions of the North Gloucestershire League Division 4 in 1952/53. Pictured are (back row): H Mogg, C Watkins, G Lewis, - ? - , R Bullock, E Hinder; (front row): T Greening, A Rigby, W Allen, D Boyce (captain, holding the cup), A Radcliffe, F Allen.

A Minsterworth AFC dinner in the mid 1950s. Pictured are: (back row) T Greening, R Steaphens, P Meadows, - ? -, R Cloak, ? Baker, - ? -; (front row): D Trigg, C Reed, (R Stephens?), M Meadows.

The Minsterworth British Legion skittles team was the main user of the new skittle alley which opened at the Bird In Hand in 1958. Mr Fletcher-Cooper, the then President of the Minsterworth British Legion, is seen here bowling the first ball.

The Royal British Legion skittles team, with wives, in the skittle alley of the Bird In Hand. Pictured are (from left to right):(back row) - John Jenner, - ? -, Arthur Jayne, Alex Kinnear, Wendy Jenner, Arthur Rigby, Muriel Rigby, Ken Jordan, Tom Greening, Jim Prosser; (front row) - Dorothy Greening, Joan Prosser, Dot Harvey, Connie Jayne.

A great time obviously being enjoyed by young people at a Christmas party in Minsterworth Village Hall in the 1950s. Among the many guests are members of the Greening and Browning families.

7

Minsterworth
At War

"Your Country Needs You"

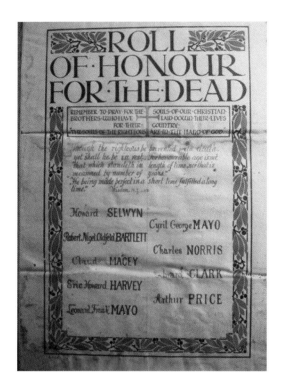

These memorials in St Peter's Church remind us of Minsterworth's losses in two world wars.

The three eldest Harvey sons Roy, Will and Eric sitting at the porch of The Redlands in 1914 just before joining the Gloucestershire Regiment bound for Flanders. Eric was to die at the Somme in September 1918.

Capt Robert Nigel Oldfield Bartlett the younger son of the Rev Charles Oldfield Bartlett vicar of St Peter's, was just one of nine Minsterworth men to lose their lives during the First World War.

According to St Peter's church magazine of the time, the Minsterworth Volunteer Training Corps, under the command of a Mr C J Watson-Munro, paraded twice during the summer of 1916. Each time, around twenty four men were involved, virtually as seen here. The Corps was the First World War equivalent of the Home Guard.

Boys of the Minsterworth Army Cadet squad marching along the main road in front of Pump Court early on in the Second World War.

During the war, a Minsterworth branch of the volunteer Royal Observer Corps provided an around the clock service to identify and report the movements of enemy aircraft. One of its members was William Vyner Ellis and when in 1943 he and his bride Joan were married at St Peter's church, his colleagues in the Corps provided the guard of honour.

During World War Two, a contingent of the Girls' Training Corps was formed in Minsterworth to provide local girls with training in first aid, fire fighting and other skills to equip them for roles in the war effort. Here we see the group mustered at the village hall with several visiting officers from London.

Enforcement of local law and order during World War Two was carried out by volunteer teams of special constables like this one serving the Minsterworth, Churcham and Highnam area. Third from the right in the front row is the local 'bobby', P.C. Evans of Minsterworth.

A party of Sunday School children visiting Moorcroft Farm in 1943. Standing next to the two land army girls is Mrs Mankellow, a Londoner working at Hygrove, and her mother. Sunday school teacher Doreen Clifton is on the far right and the group on the wagon is believed to include youngsters Kath Mogg and Chris King.

In 1944, HRH the Queen Mary, while staying at Highnam Court, visited Minsterworth to inspect a camp of young people who were helping with the local potato harvest at Highcross Farm. The bearded gentleman standing next to Queen Mary is Mr Charles Mogg.

It may have been wartime but a happy time was being enjoyed by this gathering of local youngsters in the village hall. Representatives of the Girls' Training Corps and the Army Cadet force were there in uniform.

A somewhat austere looking Hygrove House during the second World War when, known as Hampton House, it was used as the wartime evacuation headquarters of the Zurich General Accident and Liability Insurance Company. A Grade II listed building dating from Georgian times, it is now a nursing home.

This photograph shows a party organised at the village hall probably for the staff of Zurich and friends.

8

The
School

Mrs Peake was head mistress of Minsterworth school in 1907

The school went on to win the Challenge Shield for three successive years until 1909 when the school was allowed to keep it. Here we see Mrs Peake with her pupils, staff and the school trustees showing off the shield in either 1907 or 1908.

Pupils and teaching staff of the school with shields in 1909. Note the girls' white lacy pinafores and the formal suits and Eton collars worn by some of the boys.

Pupils of Group II at the school with their teacher in 1920. The lady on the left is quite likely Mrs Peake. Note the knee-high gaiters worn by the little girl in the front row.

MINSTERWORTH SCHOOL

Lots of smiling faces in this photograph of what appears to be the whole school in 1937.

Enjoying being high and dry are these children photographed in the lower school field during the serious flooding of 1947. Behind them are Street End and Snowdrop cottages totally surrounded by water.

In 1948, the school won the RSPB "Bird and Tree" essay competition and here we see the winning team of young essay writers with their winners' shield. Back row: Mrs Vyner-Ellis, Mrs and the Rev.Venables, Mr Smart, Mr East, Miss Stephens, Miss Wallace (Headteacher) and Mary Bullock; middle row: Bill Mogg, Kath Mogg, Betty Rose, Rosemary Martin, Roy Stephens; front row: Dave Browning, Arthur Rose, Cecil Boyce and Norman Bullock.

Smartly attired for the occasion are these young musicians of Minsterworth school orchestra in 1959.

In the 1950s, the school also had its own country dance team which entered area competitions in the Forest of Dean. Here we see the team of 1958.

On 12 November 1988, these local residents gathered to celebrate the village hall's Diamond Jubilee. Among those present was Christabel Mortimer who, as a little girl, had presented a bouquet to the Duchess of Beaufort at the formal opening ceremony back in 1928. On the facing page is a key to the names of those present in the photograph (as produced by Rosamond Dauncey).

KEY TO THOSE PRESENT

1	Dennis Coldwell	38	Christabel Mortimer	75	Ken East
2	Peter Arkell	39	Tim Greening	76	Mildred Robinson
3	Barbara Arkell	40	John Hockaday	77	Phyllis Clissold
4	John Jenner	41	Peter Howell	78	Jo Harris
5	Ken Jordan	42	Gwen Reeves	79	Nora Scragg
6	Cyril Hargreaves	43	John Kennedy	80	Beryl Leaper
7	Wendy Jenner	44	David Harris	81	Lucy Hunt
8	Rouex Merriman	45	Shirley Simmonds	82	Katherine Hayward
9	Roger Dauncey	46	Doug Reeves	83	Clare Cooper
10	Lou Merriman	47	Mary Cooper	84	Rosamond Dauncey
11	Helen Kennedy	48	Patrick Jenkins (Vicar)	85	Mavis Robinson
12	Dorothy Howell	49	Sue Thornton	86	Hugh Potts
13	Alan Selwyn	50	Ann Mogg	87	Muriel Rigby
14	Susan Dixon	51	Beryl Hargreaves	88	Harold Boyce
15	Elizabeth Baverstock	52	John Harris	89	Pauline Boyce
16	Ginny Hunt	53	Jim Stait	90	Donald Boyce
17	Gloria Cocks	54	Enid Smith	91	Barbara Boyce
18	Margaret Tate	55	Phyllis Pugh	92	Philip Hayward
19	Malcolm Tate	56	Dorothy Greening	93	Guy Hart
20	Mark Cinderey	57	William Gunn	94	Matthew Hart
21	Linda Cinderey	58	Nellie Moore (Wallace)	95	John Robinson
22	Carol Selwyn	59	Nellie Lyes	96	Charlotte Selwyn
23	Di Harris	60	Elsie Sterry	97	Anne Marie Mogg
24	Barry Thornton	61	Barbara Gunn	98	Phillip Howell
25	Robert Hunt	62	Mary Woodman	99	Julie Cooper
26	Mike Jenkins	63	Joan Prosser	100	David Webb
27	Pat Jenkins	64	May Meadows	101	Ritchie Hayward
28	Dennis Calnan	65	Bert Prosser	102	Gail Parkes
29	Tony Cocks	66	Jane Prosser	103	Jennifer Howell
30	Catherine Greening	67	Linda Hart	104	Edward Leigh
31	Elizabeth Greening	68	Marie Stait	105	James Hunt
32	Barbara Coldwell	69	Beverley Robinson	106	Alex Leigh
33	Maureen Greening	70	Wilfred Etheridge	107	Adam Hayward
34	Jill Jenkins	71	Linzi Blackburn	108	Lucy Leigh
35	Pauline Hockaday	72	Joan Etheridge	109	Tom Leigh
36	Gordon Mortimer	73	Jean East	110	James Kennedy
37	Felicity Karger	74	Carol Blackburn		

Acknowledgements

The photographs contained in this book are a sample of hundreds that have been made available by Minsterworth residents and others connected with the village. Indeed, thanks to the magnificent response from everyone, we hope that there will be - perhaps with old photographs still undiscovered - sufficient material for a second publication. Meanwhile for the present collection, we are pleased to acknowledge the contributions of Ann Alford, Barbara Arkell, John Browning, Reg and Margaret Cambridge, Betty Chamberlayne, Doreen Clifton, Mary Cooper, John Garbutt, Joan Gardiner, David Harris, John Hockaday, Walter Hurcombe, Joan Jordan, Felicity Karger, Tony Lakin, Dr Anthony Lynch, Mark Maycroft, May Meadows, Paul Meadows, Bill Mogg, Christabel Mortimer, Rosemary Passmore-Rowe, Liz Savage, Vera Smith, Cath Thomas, Pat Trigg, Eric Watkins and Margaret Winstone.

We also acknowledge the assistance given by the Gloucester Citizen, the Gloucester City Library and the Gloucestershire Record Office. Every effort was made to secure copyright permissions to reproduce images where this was necessary. In particular we acknowledge the permissions received to use images from *Forest To Severn Old Photos* by Humphrey Phelps, *F W Harvey, Soldier, Poet* by Anthony Boden (given by the poet's son Patrick Harvey) and *Severn Bore* by F W Rowbotham. All attempts at tracing the copyright holder for *Severn Tide* by Brian Waters were unsuccessful.

We apologise if there are errors in the captions and invite readers to notify us of any corrections or if they have additional information. Equally welcome will be any further old photographs which could be added to the existing archive and perhaps used in a future publication.